STRAWBI
& H

C000278706

JOHN IDDON

SCALA

Contents

The Toy House by the Thames

'It is a little plaything-house that I got out of Mrs Chenevix's shop and is the prettiest bauble you ever saw'.* So wrote Horace Walpole to his friend and cousin, Henry Conway, in June 1747, in a state of high excitement at finally having found a house by the river at Twickenham. The 'bauble', an undistinguished pair of small attached houses, was eventually to become one of the most famous and influential buildings in the history of English architecture.

Why should Walpole, youngest son of Prime Minister, Sir Robert, and already at the age of 30 establishing himself as a 'man of letters' and a collector, want such a house? He goes on to explain,

> Two delightful roads, that you would call dusty, supply me continually with coaches and chaises: barges as solemn as Barons of the Exchequer move under my window; Richmond Hill and Ham Walks bound my prospect, ... Dowagers as plenty as flounders inhabit all around, and Pope's ghost is just now skimming under the window by a most poetical moonlight.

 The Thames at Twickenham in Walpole's time: *View of Richmond Hill from the Terrace of Lady Ferrers at Twickenham*, watercolour by Johann Heinrich Muntz, c.1756.

◄ *A View of Alexander Pope's Villa, Twickenham*, oil by Samuel Scott, 1759.

*All quotations are taken from Walpole's collected *Letters* and his 1784 *Description of the Villa*, from Frances Waldegrave's biography *Strawberry Fair* by Wyndham Hewett, and from the St Mary's University College Archive.

The setting was superb, the Mecca of fashion and, with recent improvements in roads and carriages, now only a two-hour drive from London. Twickenham occupied a point half way between two royal residences – Richmond Lodge and Hampton Court. Its banks were lined with elegant villas (many indeed inhabited by dowagers) and not only had the greatest poet of the age, Alexander Pope, lived 200 yards downstream until his death in 1744, but the town had also attracted numerous other writers and artists. Walpole described the river as 'our Brenta', resembling the river between Padua and Venice with its string of Palladian villas. Twickenham had 'more chaises than Versailles'. His riverside villa was to be a summer retreat. Like many of his neighbours, his more permanent residence was in the St James's area of London.

During his 50 years at Strawberry Hill, from 1747 until his death in 1797, Walpole confirmed his position as one of the most notable figures of his century. He was, first and foremost, a superb letter writer chronicling the public events, social and artistic life, entertainment and gossip of his time. He became renowned as one of the century's greatest collectors and antiquaries, the creator of the first private printing press (the Strawberry Hill Press), an accomplished essayist and expert on history, painting and gardens. He was also the author of *The Castle of Otranto*, generally regarded as the first gothic novel, which was inspired by his interest in the romance and mystery of medieval castles and monasteries. There was a patriotic satisfaction that such buildings were English in origin and not Greek or Roman. So perhaps most important of all, he became known as the man who created the first significant house of the Gothic Revival.

➤ *A View of Twickenham from Strawberry Hill*, with Radnor House in the foreground, watercolour by Johann Heinrich Muntz, 1756.

➤➤ *Strawberry Hill, Twickenham, from the South*, oil by Muntz, 1758.

 Walpole's drawing showing Strawberry Hill 'before' and 'after' his first alterations between 1749 and 1750.

▼ Axonometric diagrams from 1995, reconstructing the general massing of the house as seen from the south-east in 1749 and 1754.

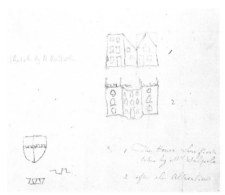

FROM CHOPP'D STRAW HALL TO STRAWBERRY HILL

Locally the house had been called 'Chopp'd Straw Hall' because part of it was built in 1698 by the Earl of Bradford's coachman. It was said he could only afford it by selling off good hay and giving inferior 'chopped straw' to the Earl's horses.

For the first few months of his tenancy, Walpole referred to the house as 'Twickenham', only discovering the name 'Strawberry Hill' when he started looking at leases in preparation for buying the house and its estate of five acres in 1749.

Walpole then began gothicising Chopp'd Straw Hall. The prevailing fashion of the time was neo-classical but in garden buildings and country villas like those along the Thames at Twickenham a greater freedom of architectural experiment was becoming more acceptable. Just as Lord Burlington had pioneered the neo-Palladian style with Chiswick House, so Walpole wrote, 'I give myself a Burlington-air, and say, that as Chiswick is a model of Grecian architecture, Strawberry Hill is to be so of Gothic'.

It also suited Walpole to retain Chopp'd Straw Hall rather than knocking it down and rebuilding from scratch. He decided to remodel the inside and 'clad' the outside as shown in his sketch of 'before' and 'after'. He clearly loved the diminutiveness of the original building, proudly referring to it as a 'toy' or 'gingerbread' house, and, when the huge Duke of Cumberland was going to visit in March 1754, imagined him straddled over the house 'peeping into the windows of Lilliput'.

The higgledy-piggledy nature of the old house would also have appealed because it already contained an element of age and 'history' and because it offered an opportunity for Walpole to develop his love of irregularity, surprise and mystery. One of his favourite words in relation to Strawberry Hill was 'sharawaggi', a Chinese word for '*want* of symmetry', and a glance at the floor plan reveals how unsymmetrical it became. It is

The ground and principal
floor plans in the 1784 edition
of *Description of the Villa*.

*East View of Strawberry Hill,
near Twickenham in Middlesex*,
watercolour by Johann
Heinrich Muntz, 1758.
The 'poodle' clipped lime
trees enabled Walpole to
enjoy the views to the river.

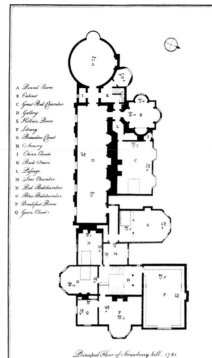

Principal Floor of Strawberry hill. 1781.

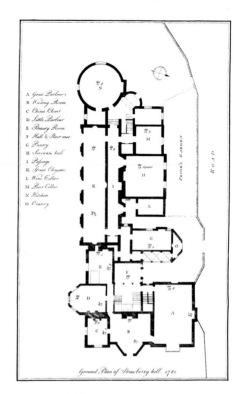

Ground Plan of Strawberry hill. 1781.

true that the close presence of the Hampton Court Road forced him to 'squeeze' his extensions westwards after 1754, but there is no doubt that the result pleased him, giving the impression of the accretions of age that generations had added.

The 'before' and 'after' illustration (see p.6) of Chopp'd Straw Hall shows the south front of the original house 'tidied up' into a balanced elevation where the main gothic features are the battlements, the gothic 'ogee' and quatrefoil windows and the finials or pinnacles.

Walpole assembled a 'Committee' to design the changes. This included his friend, the architect John Chute, owner of The Vyne in Hampshire, Richard Bentley, the illustrator, and himself. A fourth contributor, Mr Robinson of the Board of Works, dealt with overseeing structural and building matters.

The members of the Committee were amateur enthusiasts knowing little about building construction and using models of gothic design more often from illustrations in architectural books than from direct

observation (although Walpole did enjoy architectural tours to see ruins, cathedrals and his friends' country seats). Nor did Walpole want to be so gothic as to be uncomfortable. 'In truth, I do not mean to make my house so Gothic, as to exclude convenience and modern refinements in luxury'.

Victorian Gothic Revivalists such as Augustus Pugin would dismiss Walpole's gothic, especially as he did not copy in the original scale or materials (often using wood, *trompe l'oeil* or papier mâché to imitate what had been in stone) and his designs had no structural function – they were merely ornamental, described by some as 'confectionary'. Walpole coined the word 'gloomth' to sum up the effect that he wished to create. This gloomth was reinforced by the close proximity of lime trees, which he preserved and cut into 'poodle' shapes so that he could see out of the windows. He also sent an Italian called Asciotti to Flanders for painted glass. Asciotti came back with 450 pieces showing 'scriptural stories, stained in black and yellow, ... birds and flowers in

colours, and Flemish coats of arms'. These were arranged in mainly upper panes of windows throughout the house. Other features that 'gloomed and gothicised' Walpole's castle were chimney pieces, bookcases, walls and ceilings – all taking their designs from tombs and other medieval ecclesiastic features.

*North Entrance of Strawberry
Hill with a Procession of
Monks*, watercolour by
Thomas Rowlandson, 1805.

*Strawberry Hill (Entrance of
Strawberry Hill)*, watercolour
by Edward Edwards, 1781.

*An Antiquary of Strawberry
Hill*, watercolour by
Rowlandson, 1808. Is he
excited about the house,
or the servant girls
on the pie-crust wall?

Creating an Ancestral Seat

Once Chopp'd Straw Hall was converted, Walpole began to extend the house. In his *Description of the Villa* published in 1774, on his own press, he gives the dates of expansion: 'The library and refectory or great parlour in 1753, the Gallery, round tower, great cloister and cabinet in 1760 and 1761; the Great North Bedchamber in 1770 and the Beauclerk Tower with the hexagonal closet in 1776'. His final additions were the offices, built separately and to the south of the main house.

But the house was not to become a series of sterile gothic façades. Inspired by the fairy tale,

The Three Princes of Serendip, Walpole coined the word 'serendipity', the idea of encountering felicitous surprises, and the completed 'castle' achieves this: a winding route creating theatrical effects; outside views and inside light interacting; and a gradual emergence from monastic dark to more open, light and opulent spaces beyond. All give the impression of moving through an ancestral pile added to by generations of Walpoles. Apparently, a passer-by asked one of Walpole's farmers if it was not an old building. 'Yes', he replied, 'but my Master designs to build one much older next year.'

THE PRINCIPAL ROOMS

THE ENTRANCE

Visitors entered through the Great North Gate in the pie-crust wall on the Hampton Court Road. Artist and caricaturist Thomas Rowlandson, in 1805, eight years after Walpole's death, painted two cartoons of this main entrance. One (see p.9) shows an antiquarian gripping his hands with excitement at the sight of the 'ancient' building (or is it at the sight of the two young maids peering over the wall?), while a dour couple take no notice of the famous 'new-old' house beside them. The other cartoon satirises the monastic aspect of the house (Walpole called himself 'the Abbott of Twickenham') and a stream of monks queue up to enter the Little Cloister within the gate (see p.9).

Once through the gate, the visitor might feel like a religious pilgrim, with the Prior's Screen on the right, the Little Cloister ahead and a 'saint in bronze' (according to Walpole) flanked by stone bowls of 'holy water'. Actually, the saint was an angel, with slots behind its shoulder blades where once were fitted wings.

The most famous object in the Cloister was a large blue and white Chinese bowl on a pedestal, with an inscription of the first verse of Thomas Gray's mock heroic poem on the death of Walpole's cat, Selima. The cat, trying to catch a goldfish from the bowl, fell in and drowned. Gray was an old friend of Walpole's since their days at Eton together, and a companion on his Grand Tour in 1739–41. The poem concludes with this moral for cats (and women):

> From hence, ye Beauties, undeceiv'd,
> Know, one false step is ne'er retriev'd,
> And be with Caution bold.
> Not all that tempts your wand'ring eyes
> And heedless hearts, is lawful prize;
> Nor all, that glisters, gold.

◄◄
An illustration by Richard Bentley, 1753, for Thomas Gray's *Ode on the Death of a Favourite Cat*. Selima is about to fall into the tub, to the delight of the mice below.

▲
View from the Hall at Strawberry Hill, watercolour by John Carter, 1788, with Walpole's 'saints' in the windows and the goldfish bowl in the Little Cloister outside.

➤
Suit of armour, 'assumed' by Walpole to be of Francis I, King of France, in the niche on the staircase, watercolour by Carter, 1788.

THE HALL

Walpole described this as 'the most particular and chief beauty of the Castle'. The elegant staircase designed by Richard Bentley in 1753 was based on the library staircase at Rouen Cathedral. The stone-coloured *trompe l'oeil* tracery on the walls is a design copied from the tomb of Prince Arthur in Worcester Cathedral. As in many cases throughout the house, this came from a book rather than from direct observation, in this instance Francis Sandford's *Genealogical History of the Kings of England*, 1677.

Walpole wrote that his little Hall was 'decked with long saints in lean arched windows and with taper columns, which we call Paraclete, in memory of Eloisa's cloister' (from Pope's 'Eloisa to Abelard'). Walpole was striving to achieve the fashionable melancholy of Pope's poem. When a gunpowder mill in Hounslow three miles away blew up, the glass on either side of the front door shattered and Walpole wrote that his saints had been 'martyred'. This lost glass was replaced by a modern design in 2010.

The black japanned tin 'lanthorn' with painted glass gave a shadowy light from a solitary candle, contributing to the air of 'gloomth', and in a niche on the landing above, the suit of armour of Francis I gleamed. This mock-chilling setting led Walpole to dream, in 1764, of a giant mailed fist appearing from the top of the stairwell above. He woke in a fever to start writing *The Castle of Otranto*.

The staircase ingeniously unites the two new floors to the north with the three floors, with their smaller rooms, of the original house.

▲
The restored staircase, 2010.

▲►
Staircase at Strawberry Hill, print based on a watercolour by Edward Edwards, 1784.

►
A replica of Bentley's 'lanthorn' in the Hall.

THE GREAT PARLOUR

This is the first, larger, Walpole extension beyond the perimeters of Chopp'd Straw Hall. Bentley's wonderful 'original' flamboyant gothic chimney piece dominates the room, which contained the novel Bentley–Walpole designed chairs with gothic window-tracery backs. The stucco-coloured walls were originally hung with portraits of family and friends, some by Sir Joshua Reynolds. Opposite the fireplace hung a painting of Walpole's three nieces, *The Ladies Waldegrave*, 1780, by Reynolds, of whom Walpole admiringly said 'all his geese are swans. The swans of others are geese'.

The ground floor plan shows how far this Great Parlour was from the kitchen (in the base of the Round Tower) – food had to be carried outside and then back in at the main entrance.

On the landing above is the Blue Bedchamber, an example of one of Walpole's 'domestic' living rooms. This housed portraits by John Giles Eckhardt of himself and his friends. Walpole sometimes slept here when his gout was too painful for him to ascend the stairs to his bedroom on the floor above.'

View of the Great Parlour, watercolour by John Carter, 1788. Sir Joshua Reynolds' painting of *The Ladies Waldegrave* is on the right, opposite the fireplace.

The restored stained glass windows in the Great Parlour, 2010.

Detail of the restored fireplace in the Great Parlour, 2010.

The Ladies Waldegrave, oil by Sir Joshua Reynolds, 1780.

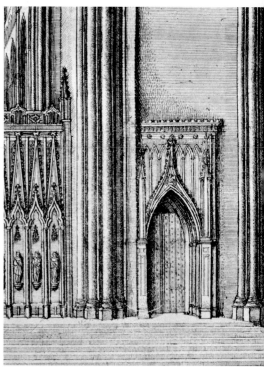

THE LIBRARY

Among the most marvellous features of the house are the pierced gothic arches of the library bookcases, designed by Chute and based on a side door of the choir illustrated by Wenceslas Hollar in William Dugdale's *History of St Paul's Cathedral*, 1658. The ceiling was designed by Walpole and painted by Andien de Clermont. It continued the theme of the Crusades suggested by the Armoury on the stairwell (where the weapons were 'supposed' to have been trophies from the Crusades) and the Saracen's head motif from the Walpole coat of arms in the Little Parlour and elsewhere in the house. Determined to make the most of his forebears' connections with the Crusades, the ceiling shows two of them, Fitz Osbert (near the window) and Terry Robsart, on horseback.

◄

Door and bookshelves
in the Library, 2010.

The Screen at Old St Paul's Cathedral, print by Wenceslas Hollar, 1658.

 View of the Library at Strawberry Hill, watercolour by John Carter, 1788. The fishing eagle, 'in terra-cotta, the size of life', in front of the fireplace, was modelled by Mrs Damer, Walpole's niece.

 Design for the Library bookshelves, by John Chute, loosely based on Hollar's illustration.

▶▶ The Library after restoration in 2010.

Chimney piece in the Holbein Chamber, 'chiefly taken from the tomb of Archbishop Warham at Canterbury', 2010.

View from the Holbein Chamber at Strawberry Hill, watercolour by John Charles Barrow, 1792, with the obelisk and river beyond. The figures in the road look up, probably entranced, at the house.

▶▶
Holbein Chamber, watercolour by John Carter, 1788, with copies of Holbein's drawings on the left wall.

THE HOLBEIN CHAMBER

This room was so named because of the portraits of members of the Court of Henry VIII traced on oil paper by George Vertue from original Hans Holbein drawings from the Royal Collection.

Bentley's beautiful screen in the room is based on one at Rouen Cathedral. The Rouen original was burnt down later in the eighteenth century so this version could almost be seen as an example of one of the 'justifications' Walpole gives in the Preface to the *Description* for listing and printing specimens of gothic features in his house: 'the general disuse of Gothic architecture, and the decay and alterations so frequently made in churches, give prints a chance of being the sole preservatives of that style'.

The chimney piece, also by Bentley, is taken from the tomb of Archbishop Warham at Canterbury. The ceiling, of papier mâché, was copied from the Queen's Dressing Room (also now lost) at Windsor Castle. A large four-poster bed with a plume of white and purple feathers on the centre of the tester would have been in the smaller part of the room.

From the bay window Walpole, or his guests, could have looked right down the leafy avenue of the old road to an obelisk by the river's edge. As elsewhere in the house, there was a play between the outside and the inside. From the lower windowpanes, the vista could be enjoyed, while the upper painted glass flickered harlequin light into the room. This painted glass is now lost, but the effect of the multicoloured light can still be felt in other rooms where the Renaissance glass survives.

➤ Monogram of Frances, Countess Waldegrave, on an iron fire dog in the Holbein Chamber, *c.*1855.

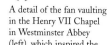

THE GALLERY

In the summer of 1763, Walpole expressed his excitement as the Gallery neared completion and his love of involving himself in the process: 'Gilders, carvers, upholsterers, and picture-cleaners are labouring at their several forges and I do not love to trust a hammer or a brush without my own supervisal'.

The fan-vaulted ceiling, based on the side aisle of Henry VII's Chapel at Westminster Abbey, is of papier mâché, and the canopies above the recesses opposite the windows are based on Archbishop Bourchier's tomb in Canterbury Cathedral.

Walpole also said that the Gallery was inspired by the historic French château of Chantilly – and there is a very unmonastic combination of gothic vaulting with the gilded fretwork, looking glass and crimson Norwich wool damask wall coverings. Gray described it as 'all Gothicism and gold and crimson and looking glass' and Walpole said: 'I begin to be ashamed of my own magnificence; Strawberry is growing sumptuous in its latter day; it will scarce be any longer like the fruit of its name, or the modesty of its ancient demeanour …'. He blamed his growing acquisitions, 'my collection was too great already to be lodged humbly, it has extended my walls, and pomp followed'.

➤ *The Gallery*, watercolour by Thomas Sandby, Paul Sandby and Edward Edwards, 1781.

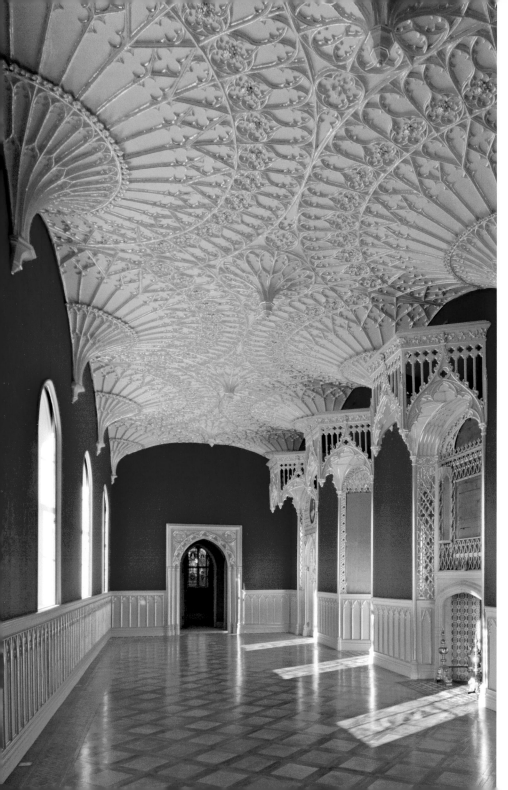

A brass inlay showing the date of the new Gallery floor 'imported' by Lady Waldegrave in 1856.

◀ The Gallery after restoration in 2010.

⋁ One of the restored canopies in the Gallery, 2010.

◀

The Tribune, 2010.

▶

The Tribune at Strawberry Hill, watercolour by John Carter, 1788.

▼

Cabinet of miniatures and enamels, designed by Walpole, made from kingwood and ivory, with figures of Peter Paul Rubens, François Duquesnoy and Inigo Jones on the pediment. Drawing by Carter.

THE TRIBUNE

Named after the room in the Uffizi Palace in Florence where the best treasures were contained, here Walpole kept his unrivalled collection of coins, medals, miniatures and enamels. Some of the latter were displayed in a Palladian style cabinet.

The vault is, according to Walpole, inspired by the Chapterhouse at York Minster. A carpet from Moorfields had a central star reflecting the star in the ceiling and a surrounding pattern taken from the mosaic in the windows. The Tribune was also known as 'The Cabinet' and 'The Chapel' but it was never consecrated, Walpole again enjoying, as with his monastic cloisters, only a theatrical sense of the religious.

◀ The fireplace in the Round Drawing Room (left) and a detail of the scagliola inlay.

▶ The Round Drawing Room after restoration in 2010, with Lady Waldegrave's stained glass windows.

▼◀ *The Round Drawing Room*, watercolour by John Carter, 1788, with the Gallery beyond and Anthony van Dyck's portrait of Margaret Lemon over the door.

▼ Door in the Round Drawing Room, 2010.

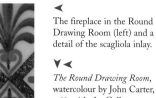

THE ROUND DRAWING ROOM

The fireplace is based on Edward the Confessor's tomb at Westminster Abbey but, as Walpole says, 'improved' by Robert Adam, one of the last architects to work on the house. The ceiling is taken from Dugdale's illustration of the rose window in Old St Paul's.

The stained glass windows in the bay and the door opposite the fireplace are Lady Waldegrave's nineteenth-century additions.

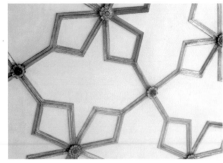

THE GREAT NORTH BEDCHAMBER

The room was begun in 1772, 10 years after the Gallery. A door in the wall to the left of the fireplace shows the roughcast outside walling of the north face of the Gallery and one of the *trompe l'oeil* windows, which would have been seen from the road before this room was added. The fireplace is modelled on the tomb of William Dudley, Bishop of Durham, in Westminster Abbey, and is made of Portland stone.

Like the Round Drawing Room, the walls were hung in crimson silk damask and the bed was of Aubusson tapestry with ostrich feathers on the corners. Six chairs were upholstered in the same tapestry. The glass closet to the left of the windows contained some of Walpole's favourite curiosities, including the gloves of James I and 'a black stone from which Dr Dee used to call his spirits'.

Collecting & Entertaining

As the house grew, so did its fame. Walpole's aristocratic friends wanted to see Strawberry Hill – a fairy castle rising by the Thames – as did everyone else. They wanted to visit the house not only because of the novelty of its architecture but also because of Walpole's famous collection of paintings, prints, books, furniture, antiquities, china, coins, enamels and miniatures. In a way, the building itself had become, like the Tribune, a 'Cabinet of Curiosities', housing one of the finest collections in the country.

Walpole would take round the people he wanted to meet and his housekeeper, Margaret, would take the rest, expecting a guinea per visitor at the end of each tour. Wilmarth Lewis, the great twentieth-century American scholar and collector of Walpoliana, imagined Walpole leading a tour of Strawberry Hill: 'hobbling ahead pointing out objects of interest, unlocking cabinets and handing people items. Dogs at heels, squirrels in windows waiting to be fed, canaries singing in cages, pots of tuberoses and heliotrope and bowls of potpourri in all rooms' – after dinner (if they were invited to stay) 'a pot of frankincense was produced'.

▼ ➤
A ticket admitting four persons to the house, 1774.

▼
The Roman eagle (first century AD) whose bill was broken by a visitor. It was excavated in 1742 within the precincts of Caracalla's bath in Rome.

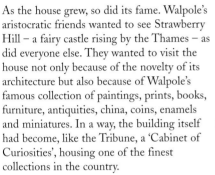

'I KEEP AN INN'

But, increasingly, Walpole found the tours a trial. He became tired of people ringing the bell at his gate requesting to have a tour of the house and initiated a system of group bookings (only from May to October, never more than four visitors a day, and no children). 'I keep an Inn' he complained 'the sign "The Gothic Castle". Never build yourself a house between London and Hampton Court. Everyone will live in it but you!'

He discovered, to his cost, that visitors 'see with their fingers', and wrote:

Two companies had been to see my house last week, and one of the parties, as vulgar people always see with the ends of their fingers, had broken the end of my invaluable eagle's bill, and to conceal their mischief, had pocketed the piece … It almost provokes me to shut up my house, when obliging begets injury.

2ˢ

This Ticket, on being delivered to the Housekeeper, will admit Four Persons, and no more, on   1774, between Twelve and Three, to see Strawberry-Hill, and will only serve for the Day specified.
N. B. The House and Garden are never shown in an Evening; and Persons are desired not to bring Children with them.

◀ Ewer 'Saint-Porchaire', *c.*1545–60, white-bodied earthenware, inlaid and glazed.

▼ *Lady Venetia Digby on her Death Bed*, watercolour on vellum by Peter Oliver, *c.*1633, after Sir Anthony van Dyck.

▼ *Lady Frances Cranfield*, watercolour on vellum by John Hoskins, *c.*1637, after Van Dyck.

Walpole's illustrated *Description of the Villa* was the most detailed account of a building and its contents that had ever been produced. However, very few were given out in his own lifetime because 'if they got the book into their hands, I should never get them out of the house, and they would want to see fifty articles which I do not choose they should handle and paw'.

Among the highlights of the collection were 670 items of ceramic in the tiny China Closet (now the bookshop), including on the centre of the mantelpiece a wonderful sixteenth-century 'Saint-Porchaire' ewer. Among contemporary pieces, in the Great North Bedchamber were two Wedgwood flower tubs designed by his friend, the artist Lady Diana Beauclerk.

The collection of miniatures and enamels was, he claimed, 'the largest and finest in any country': works by Nicholas Hilliard and Isaac and Peter Oliver were placed in and around the rosewood cabinet in the Tribune and wonderful miniatures of Sir Kenelm Digby and Lady Venetia Digby were displayed in the Blue Breakfast Room.

Walpole's picture collection, apart from the Holbeins, contained works by some of his favourite seventeenth-century painters such as Sir Peter Lely, Nicolas Poussin, Salvator Rosa and Anthony van Dyck (including a portrait in the Round Drawing Room of the artist's rather terrifying mistress, Mrs Lemon) and contemporary works by William Hogarth (including a complete collection of his prints) and the Reynolds portraits in the Great Parlour.

One of the Gallery's portraits was of
Lord Falkland by Marcus Gheeraerts. It was
this portrait, with its uncanny sense of forward
movement, that gave Walpole the idea of
having Manfred's grandfather step out from
his frame with a 'grave and melancholy air' to
the horror of the fleeing Isabella in *The Castle
of Otranto*. As with the armour in the Hall,
aspects of Walpole's own collection fed back
into his imagination for the plot of the novel.

In the glass cabinet in the Great North
Bedchamber was a much valued small bronze
'silver eyed' bust of Caligula, uncovered earlier
in the eighteenth century at the excavations at
Herculaneum and sent to Walpole from Italy
by his friend, the British Minister for Tuscany,
Horace Mann.

However, the collection was equally well
known for its eccentricities – Queen Bertha's
comb, Wolsey's red cardinal's hat, the pipe that
Admiral Van Tromp smoked during his last
sea battle and the spurs King William III sank
into the flank of his horse Sorrel at the Battle
of the Boyne. Walpole writes to Conway in
1756, joking about the 'trumpery' that
surrounds him and admitting that he was
'outbid for Oliver Cromwell's night cap' at a
recent auction and saying that his servants
think his head is turned: 'I hope not: it is all
to be called the personal estate and moveables
of my great-great-grandmother'.

Portrait of Horace Walpole (in Venice, while on his Grand Tour), pastel by Rosalba Carriera, 1741.

The Out of Town Party, oil by Sir Joshua Reynolds, 1760 (George Selwyn is on the left).

ENTERTAINING AT STRAWBERRY HILL

Walpole entertained frequently at Strawberry Hill and made close friendships with a number of charming and talented women: the Countess of Suffolk from nearby Marble Hill; Kitty Clive, the actress whom Walpole allowed to live free in a house on his estate, Little Strawberry Hill or 'Cliveden' as it was called while she was there; and the Miss Berrys, who succeeded Kitty Clive at Cliveden and whom Walpole so doted on that they were known as 'his straw-berries' or his 'two wives'.

Real wives, however, were not his orientation. As Wilmarth Lewis put it 'the feminine part of his nature was strong' and he had a number of close urbane and effeminate bachelor friends such as Chute and Gray. Then there were his literary 'clubby' friends, who were regular visitors at Christmas and Easter: George Selwyn, George Williams and Richard Edgcumbe – the threesome whose portrait, by Reynolds, hung in the Great Parlour above the fireplace. Selwyn was interested in attending public executions, dissections of corpses in anatomy theatres and all things necrophiliac. Walpole is reputed to have said of him after a particularly long time had elapsed since his last visit: 'If I'm still alive when he comes I shall be pleased to see him, and if I'm dead he'll be pleased to see me'.

Walpole entertained lavishly. He describes such an entertainment to his friend George Montagu on 11 May 1769:

Strawberry has been in great glory –
I have given a festino there that will almost mortgage it.
Last Tuesday all France dined there. Monsieur and Madame du Châtelet, the Duc de Liancour, three more French ladies whose names you will find in the enclosed paper, eight other Frenchmen, the Spanish and Portuguese ministers, the Holdernesses, Fitzroys, in short we were four and twenty. They arrived at two. At the gates of the castle I received them dressed in the cravat of Gibbons' carving, and a pair of gloves embroidered up to the elbows that had belonged to James I. The French servants stared and firmly believed this was the dress of English country gentlemen. After taking a survey of the apartments, we went to the printing-house where I had prepared the enclosed verses, with translations by Monsieur de Lisle, one of the company. The moment they were printed off, I gave private signal and French horns and clarinets accompanied the compliment. We then went to see Pope's grotto and garden, and returned to a magnificent dinner in the refectory. In the evening we walked, had tea, coffee and lemonade in the gallery, which was illuminated with a thousand, or thirty candles, I forget which, and played at whist and loo till midnight. Then there was cold supper, and at one the company returned to town saluted by fifty nightingales who as tenants of the manor came to do honour to their lord.

At other times, he would entertain his guests by having them look through the Gallery windows to watch staff milking cows (chosen, like his Turkish sheep, he claimed, for their colours and compatibility with the planting scheme) in order that they should have syllabubs fresh from the udder!

In later age, Laetitia Hawkins, a neighbour, described Walpole as follows:

His figure was … not merely tall, but more properly *long* and slender to excess; his complexion and particularly his hands, of a most unhealthy paleness. … His eyes were remarkably bright and penetrating, very dark and lively: his voice was not strong, but his tones were extremely pleasant, and if I may say so, highly gentlemanly. … he always entered a room in that style of affected delicacy, which fashion had then made almost natural; *chapeau bras* between his hands as if he wished to compress it, or under his arm – knees bent, and feet on tip-toe, as if afraid of a wet floor.

He was always a frail man. Early in 1765, his antiquarian friend Reverend William Cole, who accompanied Walpole on a visit to Paris to look at ancient monuments and bring back china, found Walpole so suffering from gout that he could not spend much time joining him in inspecting damp churches and convents. Cole thought it unjust that Walpole should have gout in 'one of the most puny, thin, delicate and meagre constitutions and frame of body this day in England', especially in view of his extreme moderation in food and drink.

The Garden & Domestic Life

Walpole started planning his garden as soon as the alterations of the house began, buying extra acres of land and planting a pleasure garden of trees and shrubs and 'sweet walks' to the south-west of the house – so 'framing' the view of the river from the house, and likewise the house from the river and grounds. The land alongside the river was sold off for housing in the 1920s, so these river vistas are now lost.

No doubt tongue in cheek, Mann asked Walpole if his garden was to be gothic too. Walpole wrote back: 'Gothic is merely architecture; and as one has a satisfaction in imprinting the gloomth of abbeys and cathedrals on one's house, so one's garden, on the contrary, is to be nothing but *riant*, and the gaiety of nature'.

In a sense, Walpole's garden manifested 'sharawaggi'. He felt that gardens had suffered from evolving from the formal garden and followed Pope in rejecting the traditional classical and symmetrical English gardens with their obelisks, pyramids and 'topiary' trees and shrubs. Like landscape architect William Kent, he 'leapt the fence' and found 'all nature was a garden'. He planted lilacs, jonquils, acacias and syringas, and established two cascades together with serendipitous 'surprises' such as a Chinese bridge, a shell bench, a chapel in the woods, a rustic cottage and a gothic screen in a Prior's Garden. When trying to explain to Mr Ashe, the nurseryman whose land was next to Strawberry Hill, the effect he was trying to gain by planting trees, Ashe replied, 'Yes Sir, I understand: you would have them hang down somewhat *poetical*'.

So, as with his architecture, Walpole was something of a revolutionary in garden design

▲
Strawberry Hill Chiefly Taken in the Year 1769, watercolour of the south-east of the house by Paul Sandby, 1769.

◄
The Great Cloister at Strawberry Hill, watercolour by John Carter, 1788.

◄◄
The newly limewashed Strawberry Hill in 2010, seen from behind the reproduction of Richard Bentley's shell bench. The greyer building to the left of the Tower is a part of Lady Waldegrave's 1850s extension.

and, as with his building, initially something of an amateur. He wrote in the early days of Strawberry Hill: 'now and then a lettuce run to seed overturns all my botany, as I have more than once mistaken it for a curious West Indian flowering shrub.' Unlike building, however, where he could create the 'instant heritage' of a baronial hall with crusader trophies, Walpole was impatient that plants were slow to mature. Speaking wistfully, to Conway he writes: 'I am persuaded that 150 years hence it will be common to remove oaks 150 years old, as it is now to transplant a tulip bulb'.

In 1753, he described the view from his castle as:

> an open grove through which you can see a field which is bounded by a serpentine wood of all kinds of trees and flowering shrubs and flowers. The lawn before the house is situated on the top of a small hill from where to the left you see the town and church of Twickenham … and a natural terrace on the brow of my hill, with meadows of my own down to the river, commands both extremities.

The aerial views showing the estate 'then' and 'now' reveal how much of the garden has been lost to College building and riverside housing in the twentieth century.

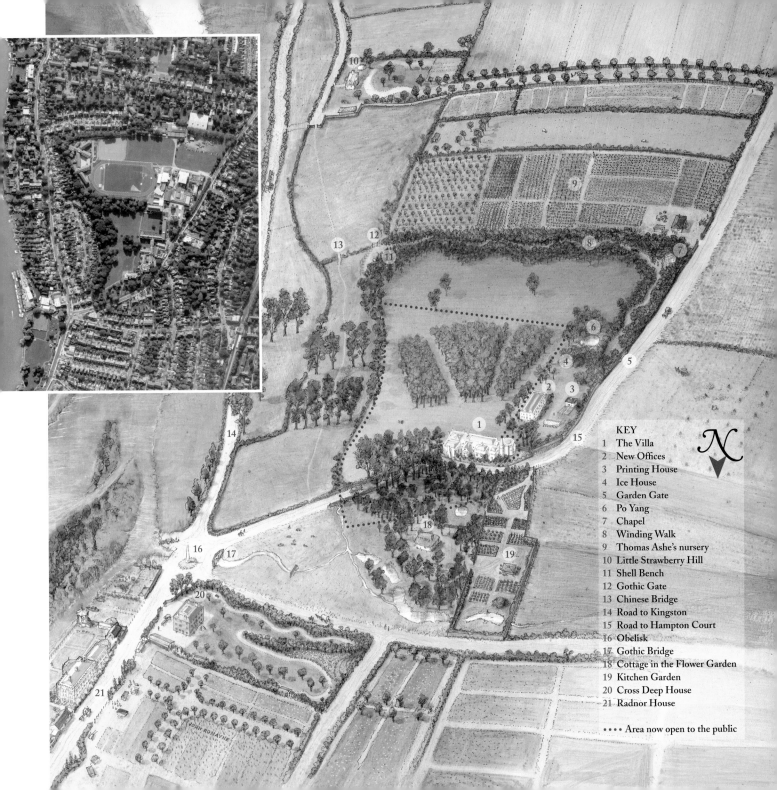

KEY
1 The Villa
2 New Offices
3 Printing House
4 Ice House
5 Garden Gate
6 Po Yang
7 Chapel
8 Winding Walk
9 Thomas Ashe's nursery
10 Little Strawberry Hill
11 Shell Bench
12 Gothic Gate
13 Chinese Bridge
14 Road to Kingston
15 Road to Hampton Court
16 Obelisk
17 Gothic Bridge
18 Cottage in the Flower Garden
19 Kitchen Garden
20 Cross Deep House
21 Radnor House

•••• Area now open to the public

N

 Walpole's gardeners at work in this *View of Twickenham and Part of Richmond Hill from the Blue Room*, watercolour by John Charles Barrow, 1789.

 The Frontispiece to the 1842 Strawberry Hill Sale Catalogue. Note the Caracalla eagle, the armour and the portrait of Lord Falkland.

 Detail of gardeners sharpening their scythes, from *View of Twickenham from the Lawn of Strawberry Hill*, watercolour by Barrow, 1791.

'A FOUNDLING HOSPITAL': DOMESTIC LIFE AT STRAWBERRY HILL

Walpole's letters are full of stories about his staff and domestic arrangements, some tragic as when his valet Phillipe Colomb announced to him that one of the servants had hanged himself in a tree on the estate. More often, however, the letters are affectionate and amusing, as when a small dog, Tonton, was sent to him by his French friend Madame du Deffand. The dog is described as 'exiling' the cat, but then hurting its paw in its excitement. Margaret, the housekeeper, tried to comfort it but, weepingly, told Walpole that it 'did not understand English'.

Walpole's kindness meant that he often continued to employ staff beyond their usefulness or competence. Those that were any good 'begot children' so that Walpole said he presided over a 'foundling hospital'. In 1759, there were rumours of a possible invasion from France and, while other estates were preparing

by raising militia from their staff, he said 'I shall not march my Twickenham militia for private reasons; my farmer has got an ague, my printer is run away, my footboy is always drunk, and my gardener is a Scotchman and I believe would give intelligence to the enemy'.

His land increased constantly even though it was difficult and expensive to accumulate, 'I have got four more acres, which makes my territory prodigious in a situation where land is so scarce, and views as abundant as formerly at Tivoli and Baiae'. By the time of his death in 1797, he had increased his original five acres to 46. Walpole left Strawberry Hill, complete with its contents, to his niece, the sculptress Mrs Anne Seymour Damer, for her life.

Detail of a gardener repotting plants, from *The South Front of Strawberry Hill*, watercolour by Paul Sandby, 1769.

Strawberry Hill in the Nineteenth Century

A CATALOGUE OF THE CLASSIC CONTENTS OF STRAWBERRY HILL COLLECTED BY HORACE WALPOLE

FARI QUÆ SENTIAT

W. ALFRED DELAMOTTE DEL.

SMITH AND ROBINS, PRINTERS,

KING STREET, LONG ACRE.

In 1811, Mrs Damer found the house too expensive to keep so she relinquished it to the eventual heir, Elizabeth Laura Waldegrave. Her grandson, John, married the 18-year-old Frances Braham, daughter of the famous tenor, John Braham, in 1839 but he died within a year of marriage. After a few months, Frances married his brother, George, the 7th Earl of Waldegrave. The marriage took place in Scotland to avoid violating the 1835 Act, which forbade marriage to a deceased husband's brother. Shortly after this marriage, George was sent to prison for six months for 'riotous behaviour'. He and some friends had got drunk during Derby week, gone on to Kingston Fair where they got even drunker and finally became involved in an affray with a policeman on the way back to Twickenham. When George came out of prison, he was short of money and felt bitterly that it was the Twickenham Bench that had committed him to the Assizes. He decided to sell Walpole's beloved collection and let Strawberry Hill rot – its empty decay would stand as a reproach to the ingratitude of Twickenham.

THE GREAT SALE OF 1842

The sale of the house contents in 1842 was perhaps the most celebrated auction of the century. George Robins, the auctioneer, known as the 'King of Puffery', had a reputation for hyperbole and fierce marketing. The catalogue, which went to eight editions and had an introduction by Harrison Ainsworth and woodcuts by Philip Henry Delamotte, was couched in language typical of Robins' exuberant salesmanship:

The valuable contents of Strawberry Hill … it may fearlessly be proclaimed as the most distinguished gem that has ever adorned the annals of auction … and within will be found as repast for the Lovers of Literature and the Fine Arts, of which bygone days furnish no previous example, and it would be in vain to contemplate it in times to come.

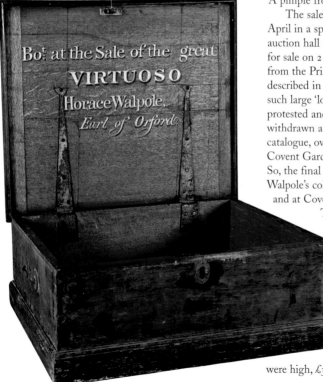

Robins was parodied widely in various lampoons with titles like 'Raspberry Hill' and 'Gooseberry Hall', which not only caricatured the shifty but eloquent Robins' style but also the small, but famous, number of eccentric 'curios' in Walpole's otherwise serious collection. Items in such mock catalogues included: 'A mouse in spirits that ran across Queen Adelaide's foot as she was going to a closet', 'The bridge of the fiddle on which Nero played while Rome was burning' and 'A pimple from Oliver Cromwell's nose'.

The sale was to take 24 days from 25 April in a specially erected temporary wooden auction hall on the lawn. However, the items for sale on 2 and 3 May – prints and books from the Print Room – were so badly described in the catalogue and herded into such large 'lots' that prospective bidders protested and the Print Room items were withdrawn and re-auctioned, with a new catalogue, over 10 days at George Robins' Covent Garden auction rooms in June. So, the final number of days' auctioning of Walpole's collection at Strawberry Hill and at Covent Garden was 32.

The controversy over Robins' marketing style and defects in the cataloguing created all the more publicity leading up to the auction and increased the number of bidders and 'sightseers' attending. A steamer service brought passengers up the Thames to the sale twice a day. The total sales' proceeds were high, £33,450.11s.9d, including £577.10s.

that was paid for *The Ladies Waldegrave*. Unknown to her husband, Lady Waldegrave bought this back along with other Waldegrave portraits by Reynolds and much of the painted glass that had been removed from the windows.

Strawberry Hill was now sadly empty, like the box inscribed 'Bought at the Sale of the great Virtuoso, Horace Walpole' (later probably used to file documents and pledges of funds for 'dealers in works of art … in necessitous circumstances'!).

In 1846, George died leaving Frances all of the Waldegrave estate, including the revenue from the Radstock coal mines in Somerset. Her third marriage, at the age of 27 in 1848, was to the much older politician, George Granville Harcourt.

LADY WALDEGRAVE'S ALTERATIONS TO STRAWBERRY HILL

In 1856, Frances decided to restore and expand the now derelict Strawberry Hill. Harcourt, knowing that on his death his estate, Nuneham Park, would go to his eldest brother, supported her plans to refurbish a house that she loved and that one day might be her main home.

She set about first restoring and adapting Walpole's original house. Her friend, and future fourth husband, Chichester Fortescue, described her relish at being at the centre of things. He saw her 'in working dress, plain black dress tucked up, ordering helpers "to put the books into the Library shelves and lend a hand to a hundred things"'. The artist Edward Lear said: 'Decision as to what she liked in art

Contemporary print of Frances, Lady Waldegrave, c.1865.

Strawberry Hill, watercolour by William Watts, c.1780s compared with, below, an 1863 calotype photograph by Philip-Henry Delamotte showing Lady Waldegrave's extension (left), heightened towers and 'Tudor' chimney pots.

was not the least remarkable of her qualities'. Frances wanted to create a larger entrance hall to accommodate the increased number of guests and did so by building a vestibule that extended the Hall to the main gate on the Hampton Road. This road was also pushed back to create a semi-circular carriageway outside the main gate. In addition, she opened up an interior route to the kitchen.

Other changes included the darkening of the Hall and stairwell by fitting the vault's quatrefoil skylights with stained glass, decorating the ceiling and Armoury niches with gold fleurs-de-lys and stars on blue ground, covering the walls in dark red flock paper, replacing the hexagonal stone tiles with colourful Minton ones and installing gas lighting. The Gallery floor was replaced by one she had bought from a villa in Paris.

Immediately, Frances began entertaining again. Chichester Fortescue sat on the lawn in the summer of 1856 after a dinner party and 'watched the house lit up, full of life. What a magical contrast to what it was'.

That year she wrote, 'Mr Cobb … and myself have hit on a splendid plan … a new building is to connect the stables (the offices) to the Round Tower'. Over the next five years, this 'link' building was completed and included a Drawing Room, a Billiard Room, a new kitchen and further accommodation for guests. Now in possession of St Mary's University College, these new rooms were grander and loftier than Walpole's, making his tower appear squat by comparison. She therefore heightened the Round and Beauclerk Towers by one and two storeys and further unified the new ensemble by the addition of 'Tudor' chimney pots to Walpole's buildings.

At Christmas 1861, Harcourt died. By 1863, Frances had remarried, at 41, Chichester Fortescue, a man of her own age who had been besotted with her for years. He served under both Lord Palmerston and William Gladstone as a Liberal Minister, his posts including Secretary for Ireland and President of the Board of Trade. In Ireland, Lady Waldegrave became known as 'The Queen of

Dublin'. When in England, Lady Waldegrave turned Strawberry Hill into the premier 'Liberal Salon' of the day hosting Palmerston, Gladstone, the Prince and Princess of Wales and everyone who was significant in the Whig establishment. *Vanity Fair* claimed that of Fortescue (later Lord Carlingford), 'history will say he married Lady Waldegrave and governed Ireland'.

By the time of her death in 1879, Lady Waldegrave had turned Strawberry Hill once again into one of the most famous houses in England. Her deference to Walpole is clear everywhere as is her ingenuity in not 'spoiling Walpole' where the joins meet. Three years before she died, Lady Waldegrave complained that Walpole, the creator of a mere 'lath and plaster' house, should get the credit for her additions to Strawberry Hill: 'Strawberry is more like a fairy palace than ever. This sounds like boasting of my handiwork, but I feel inclined to do so, as I now constantly find young people thinking that Horace Walpole made all my pet creations'.

◄
The staircase in Baron de Stern's time with dark stained wood and Lady Waldegrave's fleurs-de-lys decoration in the Armoury.

▼

The Gallery with Victorian furniture and chandeliers, 1863.

In 1886, Strawberry Hill was bought by Herbert and Julia de Stern. Among the Baron de Stern's alterations was the conversion of Walpole's Breakfast, or Blue, Room into a Turkish smoking room, with a textiled ceiling suggesting an Arabian tent.

➤

Lady Waldegrave's vestibule extending the covered main entrance to the road, c.1920s.

Strawberry Hill in the Twentieth Century

The house eventually passed on to the Baron's son, Lord Michelham, and was put up for sale again in 1923 when the Catholic Education Council bought it as a new home for St Mary's Catholic Teacher Training College (now St Mary's University College).

The architect, Sebastian Pugin Powell (a grandnephew of Augustus Pugin), designed a chapel, lecture rooms and dormitory blocks for the new College. From the lawn today, you can see three centuries of 'Gothic Revival' from left to right: twentieth-century chapel, Walpole's offices, Lady Waldegrave's 'crumacious' Drawing Room in the 'link building', and finally, Walpole's 'Strawberry'.

For a while, the College used parts of the historic buildings for the students: the Gallery became temporarily a teaching room and the Round Room was used as a linen room. When the Pugin Powell extensions were complete, in 1927, Walpole's house became the residence of the Vincentian priests, who formed the core of the teaching staff, and Lady Waldegrave's Drawing Room became the library.

◄

Students from the Art Department of St Mary's College drawing from the Antique (plaster casts) in the Gallery in 1926.

➤

The Gallery used as a classroom before the war, 1929.

WAR DAMAGE

During the Second World War, the College suffered extensive bomb damage. One night in 1940, 96 of the new College rooms were destroyed by German firebombs. According to a former Principal, Fr Kevin Cronin, who was a history lecturer during the war, a firebomb broke through the ceiling of the Gallery but was put out with a fire extinguisher by the College Matron. He remembered the College closing its doors to students in the autumn of 1940, so heavily had it been ravaged by air raids. He recorded:

In all, during the war, this place was a ruin. We dug a shelter in the grounds just under the trees on the far-side of the lawn, and we used the ground floor underneath the Waldegrave Drawing Room as a sleeping area …We were constantly interrupted by air raids – even during examinations. There was a type of enjoyment that we all felt at that time, which I have never experienced since … It emerges from this that much necessary renovation was awaiting.

CHANGES AND RENOVATIONS AFTER THE WAR

These were conducted by the architect, Sir Albert Richardson. His first task was to remove the roof over the Gallery and renew it in copper. The Library bookshelves had been grained dark brown and Richardson restored them to their original stone colour. The Tribune had been stone-coloured also, but Richardson felt that this colour only worked when full of artefacts and pictures and so, in its now empty state, he had it painted green and gold.

Lady Waldegrave's vestibule in front of the Little Cloister suffered from dry rot and had been leaking damp into the Refectory's west wall. So, the whole extension was removed and it was brought back to its appearance in Walpole's time. In 1960, a fondant pink tracery scheme was painted in the Hall and staircase and much of the painted glass, damaged or removed during the bombing, was relocated and reset (although not always in the correct places).

Strawberry Hill Restored

In 2010, Walpole's villa reopened to the public, resplendent in its former gothic glory thanks to the Strawberry Hill Trust's £9m restoration. Twenty rooms now appear as Walpole left them on his death in 1797 – a process made easier because Strawberry Hill is one of the best documented houses of the eighteenth century, extensively recorded in paintings by contemporary artists such as John Carter and Johann Muntz, and in Walpole's own *Description*.

The exterior is lime-washed again in 'wedding cake' white and the rooftop pinnacles returned to enhance the dramatic silhouette. The south-east or 'Great Tower', which suffered from both dry and wet rot, has been dismantled and rebuilt using as much of the original structure as possible. Walpole's collection of Renaissance glass has been conserved and replaced in its original locations. Where glass was lost, some replacements have been made, as with the three roundels, *Faith*, *Hope* and *Charity*, in the Library.

The interior of the house now recaptures Walpole's original concept of a journey, starting with the medieval 'gloomth' of the Hall and equally solemn gothic space of the Refectory, continuing up the stairwell to the Armoury, and into the light from the clear quatrefoil ceiling panes above. The mood then further brightens with the more colourful Holbein Chamber and finally bursts into the dazzling mirrored white, gold and crimson light of the Gallery – giving one a sense of emerging from a rich grotto into the sunlight.

Some of the features reclaimed for the first time in over 200 years include the sumptuously cleaned and regilded papier

◄ ►

Regilding and painting
in the Gallery, 2010.

▼

Comments on work
conditions in 1857.

mâché fan-vaulted ceiling and dado in the
Gallery. The window heights here have been
returned to their original dimensions before
Lady Waldegrave's enlargements, and new
specially woven crimson damask wall hangings
are based on a large-scale pattern originally
purchased by Chute in 1763.

Interesting discoveries were made when
the old Gallery wall hangings from the 1950s
were removed. Craftsmen in January 1857
(similarly engaged in restoration) wrote in
chalk on the exposed panelling of an end wall,
'weather very cold, no fires allowed'. Marks
were also found that indicated Walpole's
original picture hang.

Beneath the Gallery, the Great Cloister
arches, enclosed by about 1826 to create extra
rooms after Walpole's time, have been reopened
and the Cloister, arches now reglazed, has
become the new café overlooking the garden.

In the Beauty Room on the ground floor,
the Trust has exposed layers of past building
work and design, including the wooden
panelling of Chopp'd Straw Hall. Also revealed
are Walpole's restored windows and painted
glass, with shutters that slide (as with many
others in the house) *sideways* into the wall, to
create the effect of standing on a balcony.

The Great Parlour with its stucco-coloured walls, 2010.

The Library with Andien de Clermont's ceiling design, including the ubiquitous Saracen's head, and the restored lower panes showing *Faith*, *Hope* and *Charity*, 2010.

Other features include: a closet with nineteenth-century 'bird' paper; an anaglypta ceiling from the 1970s; and a glass panel in the floor revealing Lady Waldegrave's bell system.

As a result of the Great Sale of 1842, nearly all of Walpole's extensive collection of paintings, books, furniture, sculpture, arms and other artefacts was dispersed and, by the time the Vincentian priests occupied the house in 1923, none of Walpole's possessions remained.

The Trust wants to recapture many of these treasures in the house. For example, the Gallery will be furnished with replica sofas and one of Walpole's original gothic mirrors will be returned to the Great Parlour. Ongoing reproduction work includes the display of paintings set in the mirrored gothic tracery recesses in the Gallery, carved gothic chairs for the Great Parlour based on an original in the Victoria and Albert Museum, and a state bed for the Great North Bedchamber.

The garden is being restored to its eighteenth-century design, with the Prior's Garden recreated, a copy of the shell bench installed, an open grove of lime trees and examples of sweet walks planted. Tubs of orange trees will be put out in the summer.

Walpole once famously said (thinking, no doubt, of the papier mâché ceilings, the *trompe l'oeil* illusions of stone tracery and the lath and plaster covering of some of the building), 'My buildings, like my writings, are of paper, and will blow away ten years after I am dead'. Well, they didn't. By 2004, however, the house was on both English Heritage's *Buildings at Risk Register* and the World Monuments Fund Watch List of the world's *100 Most Endangered Sites*. Now, thanks to the Trust's work, and its many generous donors, Walpole's Strawberry Hill is here to stay.

FRONT COVER
The newly restored Strawberry Hill, October 2010.

FRONT COVER FLAP
Above: The Armoury viewed from the Blue Bedchamber, 2010.
Below: The Little Cloister, 2010.

INSIDE FRONT COVER
South façade of Strawberry Hill, 2010.

BACK COVER
Detail of the Tribune ceiling, 2010.

BACK COVER FLAP
Above: The Round Drawing Room viewed from the Gallery, 2010.
Below: The restored Hall and staircase, 2010.

INSIDE BACK COVER
Detail of new damask wall covering that has replaced the original fabric in the Round Drawing Room and Gallery.

PAGE 1
Left, top to bottom: details of gothic quatrefoil shapes at Strawberry Hill, 2010.
Right: *Portrait of Horace Walpole in his Library*, pen and ink and wash by Johann Heinrich Muntz, 1755–59.

PAGES 2–3
Lady Waldegrave's windows in the Round Drawing Room, 2010.

PAGE 48
The restored stained glass panes, *Faith*, *Hope* and *Charity*, in the Library, 2010.

© Scala Publishers Ltd, 2011
Text © The Strawberry Hill Trust
Artworks © The Strawberry Hill Trust

First published in 2011 by
Scala Publishers Ltd
Northburgh House
10 Northburgh Street
London EC1V 0AT
Telephone: +44 (0) 20 7490 9900
www.scalapublishers.com

In association with The Strawberry Hill Trust
Registered Charity No.: 1095618
www.strawberryhillhouse.org.uk

ISBN: 978 1 85759 657 1

Project Manager and Copy Editor:
Linda Schofield
Designer: Trevor Wilson Design Ltd
Printed and bound in China

10 9 8 7 6 5 4 3 2 1

ACKNOWLEDGEMENTS

The following images are reproduced by courtesy of: Bristol City Museum and Art Gallery: p.29 (left); British Library Board: p.6 (top left); © Mary Fedden and the Portland Gallery: p.43; The Friends of Strawberry Hill: pp.9 (right), 37; Henry E. Huntington Library, San Mariono, California: p.10 (bottom right); Houghton Hall, Norfolk: p.28; The Lewis Walpole Library, Yale University: pp.1 (right), 4, 7, 8, 9 (bottom left), 10, 11 (top right), 12, 15 (top left and bottom), 17 (top left and top right), 18 (bottom), 21, 22 (bottom left), 24 (top left), 25, 31, 32, 34, 35, 36, 37 (top right); © London Borough of Richmond-Upon-Thames Local Studies Collection: p.6 (top right); © National Galleries of Scotland: p.13; National Trust: p.14 (right); Private collection: p.5; © John Ronayne: p.33; The Royal Commission of the Historical Monuments of England: p.6 (bottom left); Sarah Campbell Blaffer Foundation, Houston: p.27; Victoria and Albert Museum: p.9 (bottom right)

Photographs:
© Martin Charles: p.19 (left); © Country Life Picture Library: p.38 (left); © Getmapping.com: p.33 (inset); © Richard Holttum: pp.15 (top right), 22 (top left), 23, 40 (top), 42 (top), 47; © Anthony Kersting, Conway Library: p.41; © Musée Condé: p.37 (bottom right), p.38 (top right); © National Museums Scotland: p.26 (left); © The Trustees of the Ninth Duke of Buccleuch's Chattels Fund: p.26 (bottom right); © Kilian O'Sullivan: front cover, inside front cover, pp.1 (top and bottom), 18 (top right), 44, 45, 46; © Peter Inskip + Peter Jenkins Architects: p.43; © Sharron Price: front and back cover flaps, back cover, inside back cover, pp.1 (middle two), 2, 11 (top left), 13, 14, 16, 17, 19 (top right and bottom right), 20, 22 (top and bottom right), 24, 30; © Richard Spires: p.11 (bottom); © St Mary's University College: pp.38 (bottom right), 39; © St Mary's University College photographed by Christine Jarvis: p.40 (bottom left, right and middle); © Paul San Casciani: p.48; Victoria and Albert Museum: p.29 (right); © Westminster Abbey Library: p.18 (top left); © Wingfield Digby Collection, Sherborne Castle: p.26 (top right)